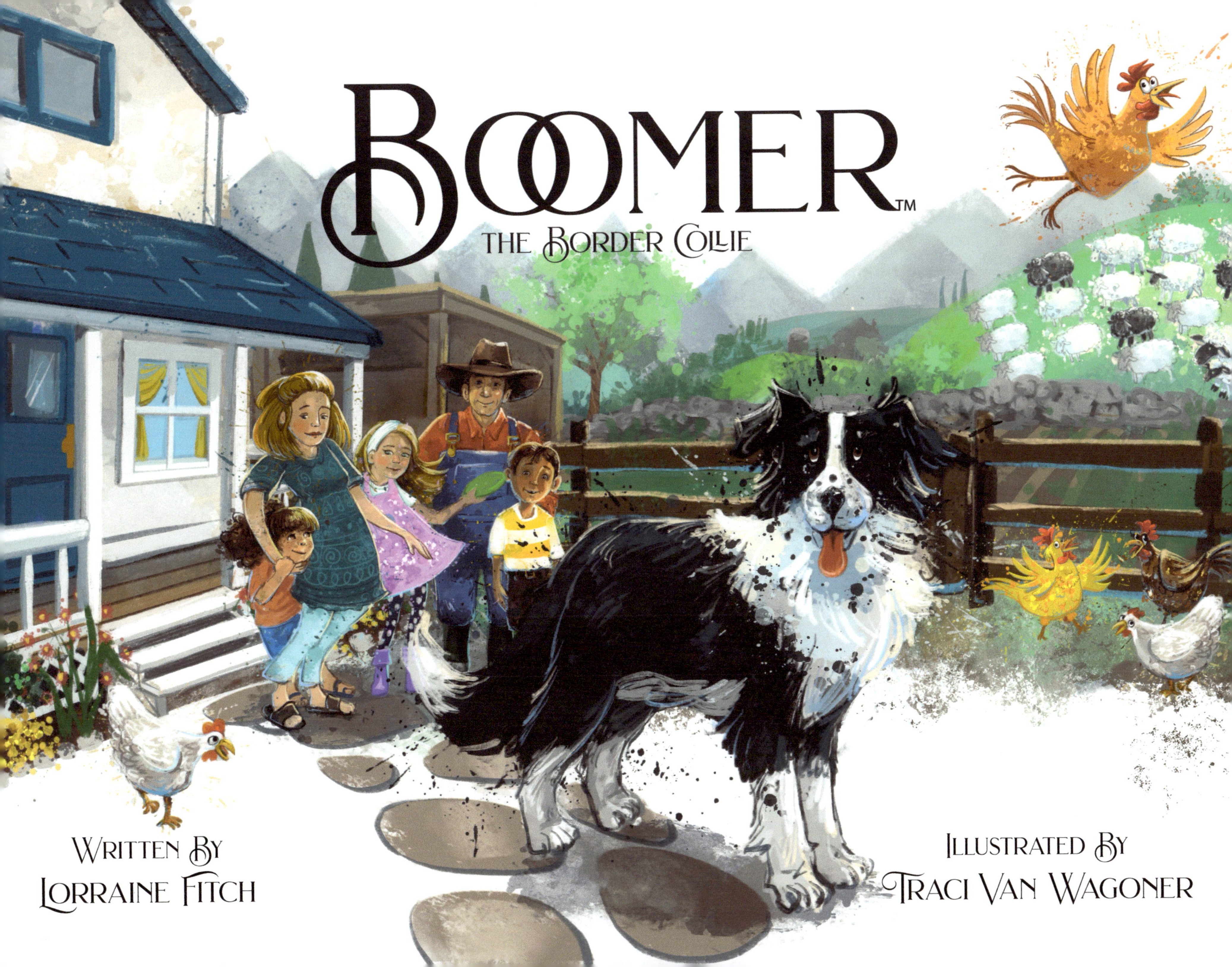
BOOMER™
THE BORDER COLLIE
WRITTEN BY
LORRAINE FITCH
ILLUSTRATED BY
TRACI VAN WAGONER

Written by: Lorraine Fitch

Illustrated by: Traci Van Wagoner
Designed by: Kurt Keller

www.bluebearstories.com
www.imaginethatdesignnyc.com
www.tracivanwagoner.com

Copyright ©2023
ISBN 979-8-218-14062-5
Lorraine Fitch / Traci Van Wagoner
Illustration Copyright ©2023
Traci Van Wagoner

To my 9 grandchildren: Hannah, Michael, Gabriel, Mary, Naysha, Seth, Slade, Quill, and Wallen, because through their love of books, I was inspired to write one about Boomer!
-LF
To all the dogs I've loved before
-TVW

This is a story about
BOOMER THE BORDER COLLIE.

He is a happy dog.

BOOMER lives on a farm with a nice human family named the O'Dans.
He knows this is their name because Mrs. O'Dan always comes to the back door at dinnertime and yells, "Oh, Dan!"
Then every one of the O'Dans come running!

BOOMER likes living on the farm because there is a lot of room for his favorite games such as chasing chickens,

jumping for the frisbee,

frolicking in the daisies,
and
just plain running.

The O'Dan pups like to play with $\mathcal{B}$OOMER.

They brush him,

they dress him up,

and they try to tickle him,
but he keeps his feet tucked under his belly so they can't reach his tickle spots.

BOOMER'S most favorite game, of course, is keeping the sheep in order. More than anything BOOMER loves to play this game. It keeps him very busy, because sheep are always out of order.

He especially likes the springtime because there are even more
sheep to keep in order.

But one day BOOMER has no fun at all. He spots a prickly pear walking through the pasture, stirring up trouble.
It is not supposed to be there. He goes to work.

Sniff. Sniff.
He inspects it more closely, and…

The prickly pear bats BOOMER right on his tender nose with nasty needles!

After much pity from the O'Dan children, Mr. O'Dan holds BOOMER down and carefully removes the needles from his nose.

Poor BOOMER decides he does not like prickly pears at all and will ignore them from now on!

The next day a different visitor comes to the farm…

The O'Dan's are at church and all the sheep are in order.
It's a peaceful morning on the farm until...

BOOMER'S ears perk and his nose twitches.
He senses danger.

He is up like a shot.
Another stranger is here. This stranger smells funny
and doesn't respect BOOMER'S place on the farm.

He warns the stranger to stay away,
but the stranger ignores him.

BOOMER charges at the stranger and nips at
him, but the stranger just growls.

The stranger heads for the quiet, orderly sheep in the pasture.
This is not good. The stranger will get the sheep out of order.

BOOMER barks wildly,
telling all the world about the unfriendly stranger.
But no one hears him except the sheep, and they begin running in all
different directions.

Poor BOOMER decides this is not fun.
He has to keep the sheep in order.

He runs frantically back and forth and nips at the sheep,
but they are too afraid.
The stranger must go away.

With all his might, BOOMER runs after the stranger growling and baring his teeth.
BOOMER grabs the stranger's ear and hangs on for dear life.
They roll and snarl all the way to the bottom of the hill.

The stranger doesn't leave. Instead he growls
louder and bites BOOMER back.

BOOMER grabs the stranger's front paw
and bites down as hard as he can.
YIPE! The stranger howls and limps off whimpering.

BOOMER did it!
His sheep are safe!

"Hooray! BOOMER, you saved the day!" one of the O'Dan pups holler.

They bandage BOOMER'S cuts and bites then give him a special bone as a reward for his bravery.

"You are a Superdog! We'll love you forever," the O'Dan pups say.

BOOMER is a hero.
But wait! Something is bothering him.

Oh yes! The sheep are out of order.
BOOMER runs up the hill and puts the sheep back in order.
He is happy again.